BE YOUR OWN BOSS: WOMAN

HOW TO BE A WOMAN WITH HER OWN MONEY

RESHELL LEE

ISBN: 9798351891927

DEDICATION

This book is dedicated to God Almighty and all the women who want to be their own Boss.

CONTENTS

1 CHAPTER ONE

Seven systems for ladies to turn into their own chief

If you're a lady who has any desire to work for yourself, all things considered this book is for you. As somebody who has been battling for endurance for a long time, this is the thing I maintain that you should be aware: Turning into your own **supervisor** can be perhaps of the most remunerating thing you will at any point do.

While there are standard working strategies for working at a laid out organization, there are no principles for business people or Presidents. There's no set in stone manner in getting things done.

So the present moment, I would be sharing seven methodologies that will help you as a lady (housewife, understudy, worker and so forth) explore this new world with a more noteworthy feeling of mindfulness, certainty, and achievement.

1. **Foster your psyche:** Turning into your own **manager** requires a change in perspective. You should begin taking care of your psyche in an unexpected way (decidedly) so you will think and act in an unexpected way. Begin by turning out to be more mindful. Carve out opportunity to recognize your interests, assets, shortcomings, how you lead, what your correspondence style is, and what your convictions are. This exercise will assist you with developing an establishment to construct yourself and make an arrangement custom-made to address your issues and objectives.

Likewise, conviction is the reason for everything. Along these lines, look at yours. Distinguish any conviction that restricts you and assess assuming it is truly evident. Let those convictions proceed to incline toward the ones that engages and free you, and this is non-debatable.

Invest energy perusing consistently. I likewise unequivocally suggest rehearsing autosuggestion and representation every day and paying attention to sound projects, for example, digital recordings, moving messages, rousing musics often.

2. **Envision horrible:** In the underlying phases of wanting to turn into your own chief, you're regularly going to consider what could turn out badly. That is not where you ought to invest your effort. In the event that you don't have the discipline to prevent your considerations from going down that way, you will make way for things to turn out badly. All in all, stretch out beyond this cycle by asking yourself forthright, "What's the most terrible that can occur?"

Try not to contemplate something horrendous that happened to another person. Consider your own life. Could the most terrible thing be that you need to go live with your folks? Also, provided that this is true, could it destroy the world? Or on the other hand perhaps it could be that you could lose all that you have? Assuming this is the case, what might you do then?

There are no ensures throughout everyday life; be that as it may, we can prepare ourselves to search for the positive qualities in all things. In this way, embrace the possibility that even the most terrible that can happen won't break you, and you can get all that you might lose and more back. Then, put that thought away and put your energy where it should be on everything that can go similarly as you need them to.

3. **Perceive there is no correct way:** In the law business, there's generally a correct way. You do things a specific way all the time no inquiries posed.

Nonetheless, when you're a business person, each circumstance, each venture, and each issue is new. There is no point of reference; in this way, you should choose what to do and how to do it all alone. And keeping in mind that there is no correct method for doing things when you're the **Chief**, have it at the rear of your brain that, through a great deal of experimentation, that there is dependably a superior way.

While that might sound startling from the get go, assuming you comprehend and embrace this thought, you will start to unwind and take on a mentality that is not quite the same as ever previously. You won't stress as a lot over being incorrectly. All things considered, you'll zero in on improving, and you will begin to make astonishing things in your business and your life.

4. **Lay out a morning schedule:** Effective ladies (and men) are particularly mindful of the work and devotion that is behind each step in the right direction. They additionally realize each critical accomplishment is the aftereffect of little triumphs achieved every day. In this way, they foster morning schedules/propensities that permit them to make every day a triumph. Consider integrating some or every one of the accompanying exercises into your morning schedule: rise early, practice appreciation (supplication), think/imagine, read assertions, or use autosuggestion, and commit time to perusing.

5. **Try not to fear disappointment:** It's frightening to consider coming up short. However, in all actuality, in the event that

you will end up being your own **chief**, you will fall flat at certain things. In the event that you're not able to go out there and come up short, you're most likely not going to do quite a bit of anything. In this way, it's anything but an issue of "on the off chance that you will fall flat"; it's "what you do when you fizzle". That is important for the pioneering outlook.

At the point when you're the **chief**, you must get back up when you fizzle. Then, you need to continue onward. At any rate, your attitude should be: "I'm terrified, yet I will get out there. In the event that I come up short, I will get up, and I will get more grounded. I will improve."

I like to say, "Dread and development remain closely connected." When you overcome the trepidation (and there's a ton of it when you're in a pioneering climate), you consequently experience the development. Thus, you need to feel the trepidation and do it at any rate. Whenever you've made it happen, the trepidation will disappear.

6. **Encircle yourself with fruitful individuals:** To find success as an entrepreneur, you should monitor who you partner with. Since, similar to a lift, your companions and partners are either bringing you up or down.

You're the normal of the five individuals you partner with the most, so ensure those individuals mirror the kind of individual you need to be. Partner with individuals who are fruitful or making progress toward progress and who have what you need.

7. **Continuously give a valiant effort:** The quest for greatness presents the very best of you as a powerful influence for anything that you are doing.

Before Jimmy Carter was chosen Leader of the US, he composed a book which discussed his graduation as a maritime official. Subsequent to completing his preparation, he went after a position in the naval force. He was evaluated by Chief of naval operations Rickover, who was a man Carter enormously respected.

The Chief of naval operations was a requesting official who told him: “Where did you come in your group at the Maritime Foundation?” With a proportion of pride, Carter said: "Sir, I came 59th in a class of 840!"

Jimmy Carter said he expected to be showered with acclaim, yet all things considered, the Chief of naval operations stood up to him with this infiltrating question: "Did you put forth a valiant effort?"

Carter mulled over everything briefly and said, “No, Sir, I didn't necessarily in all cases give my all.” After a long off-kilter quiet, the Naval commander said: "What difference would it make?!"

Jimmy Carter was so affected by that inquiry from the Chief of naval operations that he concluded that from that point on, he would constantly give his all. He even entitled his book, Why Not The Best? Furthermore, later it turned into the topic of his official mission.

Regardless of how you feel about the thing you're doing, consistently give your all. Foster an outlook that is centered on chasing after greatness. It can have the effect between missing the mark concerning your business objectives and getting things done you never imagined were conceivable.

2 CHAPTER TWO

The 16 Best Business Thoughts for Ladies

Business thoughts for ladies

Let's discuss the best business thoughts for ladies! Our reality should focus on ladies in business. All things considered, we're around 50% of the populace that is billions of ladies with one of a kind thoughts, ranges of abilities, and dreams for what's in store.

Female entrepreneurs utilize almost 9 million individuals and create 1.7 trillion bucks in deals each year. They assist with keeping the economy running while at the same time working on their own lives and enhancing better approaches to improve the world.

While any lady can begin any kind of business she has the information and experience for, here are a portion of our number one private venture thoughts for ladies who need to work for themselves.

The incredible news is that a ton of these business thoughts are minimal expense to begin, particularly in the event that you as of now have the vital abilities to get everything rolling.

1. **Instructive business thoughts for ladies**

Around 74% of teachers in the U.S. are female. You've known about male-ruled ventures instruction is certainly to a greater extent a female-overwhelmed industry.

In the event that you love engrossing and sharing information, training focused business could be an extraordinary fit. Frequently, these are the best independent companies that offer adaptability where you can pick your own hours and work from anyplace. You can likewise keep it as a one-lady activity or scale it to utilize others. Assuming you're enthusiastic about instructive business, think about a portion of these business thoughts.

a. **Coaching face to face or on the web:** Ladies with scholarly abilities can assist jokes with prevailing in their subject of decision. You can offer mentoring for grade school understudies, high-schoolers, undergrads, or even grown-ups.

b. **Showing English on the web:** Since English is a worldwide language, there's popularity from grown-ups who need to learn it and guardians who maintain that their kids should grow up bilingual. There are as of now a lot of organizations like VIPKID and Qkids where instructors can offer their administrations. Or on the other hand you can take one more course and go into business as a confidential educator on the off chance that you have the showcasing mouth or associations.

c. **Beginning an internet based course:** You can share your mastery on a specific subject by building your own courses. It's a profoundly proficient method for educating others. It's a great deal of stir front and center however whenever you've composed the materials or recorded the recordings, the majority of the task is finished. Moreover, you don't need to begin without any preparation. Since there are assortments of online course stages where you can fabricate and sell courses.

d. **Educating music:** This can be one of the most amazing private company thoughts for ladies gifted in an instrument. Publicize locally and have understudies come to you for illustrations in piano, violin, guitar, or anything your specialty is. You might actually instruct basically. There are prerequisites to show music in schools; however anybody can give private illustrations.

e. **School prep:** Because of cutthroat school confirmations, some secondary school understudies need additional assistance to get themselves in a good position. With a school prep private company, you can offer SAT coaching. You can likewise assist them with composing, practice confirmation papers, offer guidance on applying for grants, assist them with looking out for any way to improve regarding the matters they're probably going to confront their most memorable semester, and so on.

2. **Plan business thoughts for ladies**

Ladies obviously have an edge in the plan business. We straightforwardly have an "eye" for it: research shows that ladies can recognize shades of variety that seem to be indistinguishable from men. Contingent upon your other expert abilities, this can ignite a few kinds of independent venture thoughts for ladies at home. See these choices to see whether one will function admirably for you.

a. **Inside plan:** Assist individuals with making appealing and useful spaces in their homes. In certain states, beginning an inside plan business expects that you have explicit permitting.

b. **Website architecture:** It's not unexpected to see self-educated experts in the tech business, so you can without much of a stretch track down assets to show yourself website architecture and begin looking for clients. There are a few different tech abilities under this umbrella, including visual plan, UX (client experience) plan, and at times essential coding like HTML. You want to make sites appealing and simple to explore.

c. **Visual communication:** Utilize your craft abilities and visual depiction programming to make logos, infographics, notices, web flags, and that's only the tip of the iceberg. Make certain to become familiar with the customs of beginning a visual computerization business prior to beginning. Website architecture and visual computerization are incredible independent company thoughts for ladies at home. They're a fantastic choice for ladies who've proactively worked in a comparable industry and are prepared to strike out all alone.

3. **Skincare and magnificence**

In spite of ladies containing the heft of buyers in the magnificence business, just 29% of leaders and board individuals at top excellence brands are ladies.

In the main 100 magnificence organizations, just 10 had a female President. In any case, since these items are fundamentally utilized by ladies, it's a good idea for them to be made by ladies too, isn't that so?

To assist with motivating private company thoughts for ladies, the following are 50 female-possessed magnificence brands traversing moisturizers, chemicals, skincare for ladies of variety, cosmetics, and that's only the tip of the iceberg.

A little Etsy shop or a rancher's market slow down are extraordinary leaping off focuses for these independent venture thoughts for ladies. Sharpen your art with craftsman cleansers, dry cleanser, body margarines/scours, or other normal excellence items you can make at home.

Additionally, consider touchy and moderate skincare item thoughts since there are less of those around.

4. Home, life, and monetary association business thoughts for ladies

It's not only a generalization that ladies are more coordinated. Research shows that ladies are more coordinated under tension and better at task exchanging. This makes us ideal possibility to run productive independent ventures where these abilities are central. Look at the choices underneath to find assuming one will function admirably for you.

a. **Virtual help:** For some entrepreneurs, menial helpers are their life saver the ones in the background who keep everything running. Menial helpers regularly play out various authoritative assignments like noting messages, putting together schedules, doing research or information passage, and so on. You can work on them all alone as a second job, or scale up and recruit other menial helpers so you can take on additional clients.

b. **Virtual entertainment the board:** This is likewise a decent business thought for ladies who know how to explore online entertainment. In the event that you like staying aware of online patterns and can grow a following, you can be a virtual entertainment supervisor. Promoting isn't only for large partnerships. As a matter of fact, numerous entrepreneurs utilize the web to publicize their administrations and interface with their clients. Web-based entertainment the board might include everyday assignments of posting and communicating with clients on Facebook, Instagram, and even Twitter. It could likewise mean making video content for Youtube channels. You can begin offering administrations for abilities you as of now have like growing a huge web-based entertainment following for instance. Also, without a doubt, you can get different abilities as you get more insight.

c. **Accounting and bookkeeping:** On the off chance that you loved Science in school and have a skill for numbers, you could make an extraordinary clerk. Accounting is an extraordinary private venture thought for ladies since you can without much of a stretch find free accounting courses to get prepared in the right abilities. You can frequently find adaptable internet based work doing accounting for private ventures. That is the reason it's one of the incredible business thoughts for ladies at home, since you can do it as a side gig or as a regular work. Bookkeeping requires seriously preparing however you can begin by accounting while you take your bookkeeping classes.

5. **Occasion arranging**

Integrating with the thoughts above, occasion arranging is another industry that includes a lot of performing multiple tasks and organizing subtleties. For this reason it tends to be added as one of the most incredible private venture thoughts for ladies at home.

You can begin a wedding arranging business to assist ladies and grooms with organizing everything that go into the day. These incorporate blossoms, catering, DJs, photographic artists, and whatever else you can imagine.

Or then again you can zero in on different kinds of occasions. Turn into an occasion organizer for corporate occasions, business excellent openings, item dispatches, youngsters' parties, and so on. Look further into beginning an occasion arranging business.

6. **Application improvement (An extraordinary business for ladies in tech)**

Coding abilities are not difficult to master free of charge on the web and have a wide assortment of valuable applications (seriously). To utilize them to work independently and construct projects, you could appreciate zeroing in on application advancement programming dialects.

You can assemble any sort of application you need. In any case, if you need to add a female-driven contort, there are a lot of supportive applications worked by ladies, for ladies.

Contemplate the little issues you experience every day as a lady and how an application could tackle them. Then, at that point, you could construct one connected with individual wellbeing, making new female companions, customizing skincare in view of information, and so on.

7. **Really focusing on creatures or kids**

Do you cherish creatures or children? Get compensated for it! More than 92% of childcare laborers are ladies since mothers for the most part really like to leave their children with female parental figures. Beginning a home childcare can be an incredible business thought for ladies.

You'll have to get the legitimate permitting for your state, set up an inviting consideration space, and consider how you'll deal with the thousand things that children can require.

In the event that you're a pet person or a creature darling, there are a lot of ways of transforming shaggy companions into fuzzy clients. You could offer administrations like pet sitting or preparing. You can likewise begin a canine strolling business by utilizing an application or site.

8. **Food administration**

Got ability in the kitchen? Need to practice your cake brightening chops more frequently than a periodic birthday? Begin a food-focused business!

Simply remember that with any food business, you'll be represented by your state's relevant prerequisites on food handling. You could need to lease a business kitchen or get your home kitchen investigated before you can begin making deals.

a. **Baking business:** Make cakes for exceptional events, take orders for treats and cupcakes, heat new portions of bread, and so on. This is one of the most mind-blowing independent venture thoughts for ladies who love being imaginative with making prepared merchandise. Furthermore, it can take a few structures. You could get an actual customer facing facade and begin an authority pastry shop, offer specially made heated merchandise for pickup or conveyance, or even sell them on the web on the off chance that you're certain they'll transport flawless.

b. **Cooking:** You can likewise begin a locally situated providing food business to plan starters and feasts for different kinds of occasions. On the off chance that you can possess a specialty market that is uncommon in your space you'll be bound to stand out as another business. Instances of new business sectors you can investigate are sans gluten or vegetarian cooking.

c. **Food truck:** Take your recipes out and about by putting resources into a portable kitchen a food truck! These can be expensive to fire up, so testing your recipes and nearby interest on a more limited size first may be savvy.

Obviously, they're still a lot less expensive than an undeniable café and can give you more opportunity with the business.

9. **Photography**

Returning again to the eye for plan and variety, those are both engaged with creating an incredible photo. The cash in photography is generally in occasions like weddings, and it very well may be a troublesome industry to enter. In any case, it likewise makes an extraordinary side business thought for ladies, since you can plan wedding or picture meetings on ends of the week regardless keep your everyday work. More deeply study beginning a photography business.

10. **Running a web-based store**

There are lots of web-based business thoughts for ladies at home, however one that offers bunches of adaptability and low startup costs is running a web-based store. With a web-based store, you can use the force of the web. You can get your items out into the world without leasing an actual retail customer facing facade.

You can maintain your business through a laid out web based business website like Etsy, Amazon, or eBay. In any case, you can decide to fabricate your own site on a stage like Shopify.

The greatest inquiry is what to sell and that part's doing you. You can sell your own created things, flip carport deal finds, or configuration clothing whatever there's an interest for.

11. **Composing/contributing to a blog**

Did you generally get 'A' on your school papers? You could have ability for the composed word! Use it to begin an independent composing business or run and adapt your own blog on a point you're enthusiastic about.

For each incredible client, you could experience 10 who need to pay a penny for every word. You could start out composing super charming substance about water channels and whether black-top or cement is better for carports. It's all important for the excursion!

Assuming you go writing for a blog course, it requires investment to get laid out in your specialty. It takes a ton of work and learning Website design enhancement before your blog entries begin showing up in web search tool results.

Actually at that time could you at any point transform your blog into a fruitful business and a wellspring of income.

12. **Travel-based organizations**

Travel organizations can make fun and energizing professions and are the absolute best business thoughts for ladies! In the event that you appreciate conversing with individuals, exploring, or examining realities and history about different spots, you should work in movement and the travel industry. Check whether one of these choices seems like a solid match.

a. **Travel organizer:** In the event that you love to design things and have a ton of information about extraordinary travel arrangements and flights, you may be keen on being a movement organizer or travel planner. Assist clients with booking incredible excursions, flights, or transportation, and by and large ensure that their get-away goes without a hitch.

b. **Local escort:** On the off chance that you live close to a traveler objective region and appreciate meeting new individuals, you can begin your own local escort organization! Show visitors renowned destinations and eateries, and answer their inquiries. While it might require investment to get everything rolling, this can be a wonderful method for bringing in cash for the perfect individual.

13. **Workmanship and inventive business thoughts**

Assuming you love to make things or are exceptionally imaginative, there are a lot of business thoughts for that. There are a lot of things to work in, as well. See these choices to see whether one will function admirably for you.

a. **Sell wall workmanship:** Have good thoughts for ornamental wall craftsmanship? You can make your own plans and afterward sell them on the web. Individuals are continuously searching for remarkable ways of embellishing their homes, so this can be one of the most outstanding independent venture thoughts for ladies. You can make plans utilizing a PC and afterward sell the picture on the web, or on the other hand in the event that you like, you can draw or paint novel craftsmanship. In the event that you decide to go the PC course, you can utilize a program like Canva to make lovely fine art. What's more, to paint or draw your own craftsmanship, you can sell it on the web or even at a market or a store.

b. **Cosmetics craftsman:** On the off chance that you're perfect at cosmetics and skill to showcase your administrations, you could do well as a cosmetics craftsman. You can do cosmetics for theater, occasions, films, and the sky is the limit from there. For this kind of work, it's critical to continue fostering your cosmetics abilities through taking courses, watching recordings, and loads of training.

14. **Wellness organizations**

Wellness is a thrilling industry that assists individuals with remaining in shape and happy about themselves. Assuming you're energetic about remaining sound, think about a portion of these business thoughts.

a. **YouTube wellness recordings:** On the off chance that you have a particular wellness expertise, similar to heart stimulating exercise or yoga, you can make YouTube exercise recordings. It's one of the most amazing thoughts for ladies at home since you can work from anyplace. You'll have to begin a YouTube channel, do explore, market your channel, and make certain to make intriguing recordings with great example plans.

b. **Fitness coach:** Many individuals need to get in shape and like the inspiration of having a fitness coach. Mentor your clients to turn into their best selves by making exercise arrangements and giving supportive counsel and ideas.

15. **Online Business**

As you hope to enter the positions of the present fruitful business visionaries who are perseveringly serving a great many clients all over the planet, it is indispensable to find a web-based business thought that matches your abilities or assets. All things considered, you're probably going to associate better with your clients opposite addressing their requirements in the most ideal manner.

Exploring the right business thought for yourself might appear to be a big deal responsibility, yet you can definitely relax. There are a few incredible models currently in progress. To guarantee you're in the loop, I've ordered the main 20 web-based business thoughts that you can begin immediately, with top to bottom clarifications of what every one involves to assist you with working for yourself as a lady.

a. **Partner advertiser/Affiliate marketer:** On the off chance that you've constructed a significant internet based crowd or following, you might need to investigate member promoting and how you can utilize it to adapt your substance. As a member advertiser, you'd collaborate with a business to showcase their items or administrations by prescribing or sharing them to your fans. Member advertisers procure a commission each time they convert any of their devotees into buying the brand's items through a special outside reference, known as a subsidiary connection. While thinking about which associate program is appropriate for you, search for one that suits both your inclinations and that of your interest group. Attempt to find a brand that you trust in or would be glad to support. What's more, twofold check that the item or administration that they offer has a sufficient interest. There are many offshoot programs out there, including Expertnaire, Selar, AffiliatedNg and so forth Partner Program, so you should pause for a minute to investigate them before you connect.

Whenever you're joined, you can start advancing the offshoot content close by your everyday materials which your adherents have generally expected. There are various ways of elevating your member items to your perusers without appearing to be too malicious. One strategy is to have a go at integrating the item proposals into a blog entry, instructional exercise or video utilizing pertinent and connecting with content. Be innovative and consider better approaches to adjust your advertising procedure to return the most benefit.

b. **Outsourcing entrepreneur:** Some entrepreneurs might like running a web-based store, yet don't believe or have the limit should store stock. For these cases, there's an elective way while thinking about how to begin a business on a careful spending plan. With outsourcing, you can sell items on your business site without dealing with your own stock. All things considered, you can send clients' requests to an outsider retailer. This takes out the gamble of loading up on expensive items, or figuring out that the items in your stock are as of now not attractive. Without expecting to take care of a distribution center or an alternate actual area of your stock, you can maintain your outsourcing business from any place you have WiFi. This additionally permits you to grow your item offering, since you won't be restricted to what's in a stock. Moreover, working an outsourcing business liberates you to change your product by testing and testing with it, keeping your contribution up with the most recent patterns. In the case of something isn't offering, you'll have the option to change your contributions on the spot.

c. **Facebook promotion subject matter expert:** What individual hasn't utilized Facebook as of now? In the private venture area, in any case, there are numerous veteran entrepreneurs who aren't effectively taking advantage of the plenty of assets that the online entertainment goliath brings to the table. The answer for some is to recruit a specialist on Facebook publicizing. Known as Facebook promotion trained professionals, they want to team up with clients to assist them with arranging, measure and execute paid advertising efforts on Facebook. As a recruited master, you'll have the option to assist your clients with streamlining their computerized showcasing and publicizing, permitting them to arrive at their target fans. Facebook advertisements are designated to clients in light of area, socioeconomics, and interests, making it more straightforward to track down the right specialty.

d. **Resume and introductory letter author:** Composing resumes and introductory letters is popular. Despite the fact that the run of the mill word count for an expert resume or introductory letter doesn't arrive at in excess of 400 words, crafted by a resume and introductory letter essayist is fundamental and never-ending. Your main interest group is any singular searching for a task, leaving you allowed to work with quite a few clients. Make certain to give effective composing tests you've chipped away at in the past to expected clients, or offer connects to online resume sites that you've made. This permits you to flaunt your abilities and rich industry language for any market or specialty.

e. **Digital book writer:** While few scholars figure out how to get distributed in the course of their life, many new writers are now making their digital book debut in the midst of the computerized book market blast. Independently publishing your book has never been more reasonable or powerful, utilizing various choices including Apple Books, Smashwords and Amazon, which will assist you with the after creation parts of circulation and deals. Consider putting resources into a supervisor or editor and an artist to make your book more attractive. As an author, breaking into the class of digital book writer is one web-based business thought that could be useful to you prevail in your industry. For additional enquiries on Amazon kdp hit the link. This is my profession, so I will not be one-sided: it is an extremely fascinating business to begin.

16. Anything that accommodates your abilities and interests is an incredible business for ladies

Try not to drive yourself to fit the example of what you figure ladies in business ought to do or be. If you have any desire to begin a finishing business, become an individual culinary expert or fitness coach, or another traditionally male-overwhelmed space, and you have the information to make it turn out let it all out.

Very much like the instance of Mrs. Onokpite Agbaduta, who is a Nigerian mother that prepared her children up to college level as a "transport driver". The 59 years of age female driver who handles highway courses, enlivened numerous web-based entertainment clients with her account of courage and she was granted by the Alice Ajisafe Establishment on July 22nd 2022 for that. She turned into a transport driver after the demise of her better half in 1991.

You might confront a greater amount of a daunting struggle and experience individuals who misjudge you, however somebody needs to change the ladies in-business measurements. These productive business thoughts for ladies are only an aide and can assist you with creating much more thoughts!

Evaluate one of these best business thoughts for ladies!

There could be no greater time than now to make a move on the above-recorded business thoughts for ladies and then some! What's more, recall, you can work for yourself as a lady!

3 CHAPTER THREE

Ten (10) justifications for why ladies should be monetarily autonomous

With the sort of average cost for many everyday items that the ongoing age needs to tolerate, it's a good idea that each functioning age part procure some piece of it. Monetary freedom is the capacity to make money. Each lady must be monetarily free. Nonetheless, an interesting point is that ladies outlast men by and large and subsequently a significant number of them should carry on with their resigned lives alone.

In these changing times and rising expansion, each individual from the family should be monetarily free. Such countless ladies, particularly in India, penance their vocations once they get hitched. The greater part of these ladies are taught and fit for acquiring great. Be that as it may, because of the tension from their families and society, they find employment elsewhere after marriage or in the wake of becoming a mother. Here's the reason each lady should be monetarily free, wedded or not.

1. **To pre-empt crises:** Each family should be ready for a possibility. Cutbacks are more incessant, positions aren't really secure nor is life. Assuming the spouse is the sole bread worker, with the wife and children being subject to him, then, at that point, there is excuse to be stressing out for the family. Alarm will in general result in the time the man gets another line of work. With most families risking different EMIs, it's a good idea for the woman of the house to likewise hold down a task.

2. **To meet the increasing cost for many everyday items:** Expansion, obviously, has risen observably over the most recent couple of many years. To claim a fair home, send

your children to a decent school and carry on with a better than expected way of life has become extremely high. Subsequently, 2-pay families positively charge better. Ladies who are monetarily free cannot just add to the regular costs of the family, yet additionally help to meet the family's monetary objectives.

3. **To feel mindful and encourage everyone:** Monetarily free individuals are equipped for taking their own choices and don't need to rely upon anyone. This expands their dignity and makes them more certain to confront any sort of circumstances throughout everyday life. Numerous ladies from moderate foundations with dreams and goals rely upon their accomplices or guardians for their satisfaction. Being monetarily free, will empower them to independently satisfy their desires, improve their ranges of abilities, go for an outing with companions, or in any event, purchasing things that they need, etc.

4. **To quit feeling subordinate:** Nobody ought to need to endure aggressive behavior at home or misuse, considerably less on the grounds that they're monetarily reliant upon their accomplices. In this manner, it is critical that each lady turns out to be monetarily autonomous so they never need to feel defenseless throughout everyday life.

5. **To be a good example:** A lady who can uphold the requirements of the family monetarily, socially, sincerely, etc is a good example for her youngsters to show them that orientation inclination is made by the general public and amounts to nothing when a lady is solid, certain and secure with herself. The kids gain as far as they tell. Assuming children see that their moms are monetarily

autonomous, they will likewise figure out the worth of cash and be enlivened to be independent in life when they grow up.

6. **Spending limit of the family:** A monetarily free lady can uphold her family inside and out. With steep expansion, it is essentially difficult to have a decent existence with only one individual procuring.

7. **Confidence:** The self esteem of ladies is frequently disregarded. At the point when a lady is procuring, she doesn't have to ask her better half for cash for her costs.

8. **Deserve admiration from the relatives:** Monetarily free ladies deserve admiration from each individual from the family. Ladies, who are monetarily subject to their families, frequently face slight. Indeed, even the family members and neighbors regard a monetarily free lady.

9. **Can bear upping to barbarities and foul play:** Ladies who are not monetarily free, can't tolerate upping for themselves or some other persecuted individual in the public eye. The spouse or other relatives might take advantage of the monetary reliance of ladies to carry out abominations on them.

10. **Expanded Fearlessness:** Monetary Autonomy gives self-assurance. On the off chance that the lady of a house is fearless, she can settle on better choices for her loved ones.

It is critical for all ladies be it hitched, single, isolated, bereaved or separated to be monetarily autonomous. Be that as it may, it is significant not to monetary freedom with monetary security. A regularly scheduled pay check in your ledger alone can't deliver you fit for meeting your monetary objectives as a whole. It is the way you plan and deal with your funds which will bring about fulfillment of objectives further down the road.

4 CHAPTER FOUR
Financial Freedom Quotes to stay motivated

In order for you to stay motivated and stay on track **been your own boss as a woman**, below are 10 financial freedom quotes to keep you motivated.

1. "Being rich is having money; being wealthy is having time." - **Margaret Bonnano**

2. "If you want to be financially free, you need to become a different person than you are today and let go of whatever has held you back in the past." **Robert Kiyosaki**

3. "Your economic security does not lie in your job; it lies in your own power to produce to think, to learn, to create, to adapt. That's true financial independence. It's not having wealth, it's having the power to produce wealth." **Stephen Covey**

4. "To become financially independent you must turn part of your income into capital; turn capital into enterprise; enterprise into profit; turn profit into investment; and turn investment into financial independence."**Jim Rohn**

5. "Believe that you are worthy of financial freedom. Do something you love and then all you ever have to do is be yourself to succeed." **Jen Sincero,** You Are a Badass at Making Money: Master the Mindset of Wealth

6. "Whenever we spend money instead of investing it, we are actually taking from ourselves; we are taking both the time we spend to make the money and the future freedom it can buy."**Grant Sabatier**

7. "Financial stability is much more about doing the best with what you have and not about achieving a certain level of income." **Erik Wecks**

8. "To achieve what 1% of the world's population has (financial freedom), you must be willing to do what only 1% dare to do...hard work and perseverance of the highest order." **Manoj Arora**

9. "The key to financial freedom and great wealth is a person's ability to convert earned income into passive and/or portfolio income." **Robert Kiyosaki**

10. "Remember to remember your power everything you've learned with these steps to financial freedom and put it all into practice every day, because in the grand scheme of life, you'll never really know how things are meant to turn out until they turn out." **Suze Orman**

ABOUT THE AUTHOR

Is it true that you are anxious to fill your living with more amicability, power, authority, and euphoria?

We should be moguls' nuances a reasonable, reachable, plausible, step by step approach to building the establishment, point of support, backing, conviction, and plan you truly need to have your flourishing and turned into the tycoon you need to turn into.

Only 10% of the world's moguls are women, making it difficult for women to utilize the money related influence that will make getting through correspondence. Whatever is keeping you from having seven figures in the bank – whether it's shaky sureness, data openings with respect to developing long haul monetary steadiness systems, a powerlessness to embrace achievement, a junky standpoint about cash (it's alright, we've all been there!), or simply not knowing where to begin – this book lets you know the most ideal way to address every barricade in your way, show up, and try to please.

With regards to your cash and funds, would you say you are a maiden in trouble? Now is the right time to claim your monetary life similarly as to your profession and wellbeing. Assuming that the entire thought of monetary arranging panics you, working for yourself is great. Practicing savvy cash choices ought to be regularly for each lady who thinks often about their monetary future. To shape great.

Inside this book, you are going to learn:

- Seven systems for ladies to turn into their own chief
- The 16 Best Business Thoughts for Ladies
- Business thoughts for ladies
- Ten (10) justifications for why ladies should be monetarily autonomous
- Financial Freedom Quotes to stay motivated

This present time is the best opportunity to foster a totally new demeanor about cash, ensure your power, and gather the money related security that you truly need and legitimacy - so you can stop basically making due, and start prospering. We should start off.

www.ingramcontent.com/pod-product-compliance
Lightning Source LLC
LaVergne TN
LVHW041301150826
845673LV00008B/2686
* 9 7 9 8 3 5 1 8 9 1 9 2 7 *